Hey, Heidi — that's how you spell your name right?

To the point — I kinda

Ron Russell

like you... I like when you smile, showing those pearly teeth

The Murder Of Jimi Hendrix

320 349 1509

The Murder of Jimi Hendrix

Ron Russell

With

Armond Blackwater
&
Jillian Martineau

~ Ron Russell ~

The Murder of Jimi Hendrix

Copyright © 2000 – 2017
Ron Russell
Armond Blackwater
Jillian Martineau

All rights reserved.
Including the right of reproduction
In whole or in part.

FIRST EDITION, 2017
Café Beat Publishing
New Orleans

Manufactured on planet Earth by Human Beings.

Cover Photos by Armond Blackwater

The Murder of Jimi Hendrix

This book is dedicated to Sue Wood.

"Romans 9:1 – It was All the Lords doing, to Yahweh be All the Glory" – Ron Russell

The Murder of Jimi Hendrix

"Jimi Hendrix was murdered!"

Our mutual friend Richard Yager brought Ron Russell to the Cafe' Be At Studio in Tampa in 1999 saying that I really "needed to hear this guy's story".

I was dubious. Over the course of 7,000 gigs, I've heard hundreds of unbelievable stories.

Weird, crazy stories that the tellers swore happened to them, only, I heard the same story by multiple tellers. They were common road stories.

Do you how many Southern drummers jammed with the Allman Brothers? All of them.

With Ron Russell, there was a difference. I, like most, accepted the official proclamation that Hendrix died of a drug overdose. He joined Janis Joplin and James Douglas Morrison in the pantheon of Rock Stars that died at age 27.

Ron Russell had a different take on Jimi's death. Ron insisted that Jimi was murdered and he needed to share the facts of his experience.

~ Ron Russell ~

The Murder of Jimi Hendrix

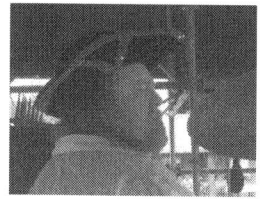
If it was just some guy telling me this story on a bar stool in a local pub I'd have listened politely and probably bought him a drink or three for entertaining me.

But there was something different about Ron Russell. He exuded an aura of truthfulness. The level of detail that he related was uncommon. I asked many questions as he went along. His memory of the events was crystal clear. His descriptions were chilling at times. It was clear that he truly believed that Hendrix's death happened exactly as he described.

I'm not a journalist. I've never claimed to be. I studied Creative Writing in college, not Journalism. But I do confirm stories before I publish them. I also talked to my lawyer who advised against publication of these potentially libelous claims. "They can't sue me if it's true, can they?" He said, "No, but you're risking everything." I don't care about money or things. I care about truth.

The Murder of Jimi Hendrix

I did more research on this story than any previous. I talked to people that knew Ron at the time of the incident. My friend, Brad Trumbull of Thoroughbred Music, played Hammond Organ onstage of the Men's Garden Club in Tampa, Florida, with Jimi while Ron drummed.

I spoke with the lady who had been Jimi's road manager, Lore Pearson, on his final European tour. She confirmed the story, "It all fits.". Ron met with Lore to share their memories of Hendrix. Ms. Pearson reported back to me that she was 1000% convinced that Ron was telling the truth.

Add to all that the fact that Ron had a great career going as drummer for Bertie Higgins' Band of Pirates, was a session drummer, and on call for bands such as the Beach Boys and other National acts. Ron had everything to lose by telling his story and nothing to gain.

I received numerous comments on the article, most questioning my sanity and one veiled threat that included a dark devilish face with glowing red eyes. I took them in stride.

~ Ron Russell ~

The Murder of Jimi Hendrix

However, I was never contacted by the surviving principal named as one of the two murderers. I was never sued. Yet, I know that he read the story and was fuming. He was the one that sent the veiled threat – a red and black devils face.

I also received an email from Eric Clapton. Yes, *The* Eric Clapton. His message was simply, "This is the worst piece of rubbish I've ever read." I was blown away. First, that *The* Eric Clapton had taken time to read my story and, second, that he ranked it as "the worst piece of rubbish" he'd ever read.

Wow. I'd have been honored if I'd fallen into the Top 100 pieces of "rubbish" he'd ever read, but to me Number 1 on his list? I felt majestic.

The story died down and was mostly forgotten. That was until James "Tappy" Wright published his autobiography "**Rock Roadie**". Therein, Tappy described a conversation that he had with his close friend Michael Jeffery (the notorious manager for Jimi Hendrix) that paralleled Ron Russell's story down to the minutest of details.

The Murder of Jimi Hendrix

Tappy had never read my story or heard of Ron Russell or me. He merely related a story that Jeffery told him over brandy in 1973 as he unburdened himself of years of guilt. Their conversation occurred a few months before Jeffery died in a mysterious plane crash.

I contacted Tappy. We conversed and he confirmed Ron's description of the events. We got together for dinner at the Hard Rock in Orlando and talked until closing.

Tappy Wright was a fountain of great stories including his recollection of his closest friend, Michael Jeffery.

That's the background, now here's the story.

- Armond Blackwater

Mini-Bio

Ron Russell was born January 10, 1951 in Chicago Heights, Illinois.

Ron discovered his passion in life at age 6 while witnessing a Gene Krupa concert with his father.

Ron's family moved to Satellite Beach when his father secured a job at NASA at the beginning of the Space Race.

Ron followed his calling a drummer, studied hard, and eventually joined the Satellite Beach High School Marching Band.

The 60's spawned the era of garage bands. Ron and friends Wally Dantz and Dave Fiester formed the band Raindriver.

Raindriver started out playing high school dances, proms, and weddings on the Space Coast. Practice and playing constantly produced a very tight unit in a short time.

The Murder of Jimi Hendrix

Upon graduation, the band decided to head to the larger venue of the Tampa/St. Petersburg area where they gained immediate acceptance, building a solid following of fans.

Raindriver's popularity led to a gig hosting the weekly Sunday jams at The Tampa Garden Club on Bayshore Drive in Tampa. The venue, established in 1926, hosted a variety of events: Weddings, Debutante Balls, Cotillions, Sweet 16 Parties, Political Rallies, and a weekly Sunday afternoon jam session that attracted elite players from the Tampa Bay area.

~ Ron Russell ~

Raindriver Sunday

Raindriver's success in the local club scene led to a regular Sunday gig hosting a jam session that The Men's Garden Club in Tampa. It was there that Ron Russell jammed with the man many consider to be the greatest guitarist of all time.

It was break time for the band. Ron wandered off to sit in the cool of a giant oak on a hot August afternoon.

Ron felt a warm rushing wind surround him. He smelled a scent that was wonderful, fragrances of rose, peach, and magnolia among others that were hard to describe. The scent always signaled that his "best friend" was about to speak.

"Go talk to Jimi. You have something in common," the voice said. Ron rose and started walking toward Jimi Hendrix.

"What do we have in common?"

The voice merely repeated, "Talk to Jimi. You have something in common."

The Murder of Jimi Hendrix

Hendrix watched Ron curiously as he approached. When Ron got close enough, Jimi asked him, "Man, are you crazy?"

Ron replied, "No, I'm a rather intelligent person. Why?"

"Then, are you a ventriloquist or something?" Jimi probed further.

A large smile broke on Ron's face, "You heard the voice, didn't you?"

Jimi responded, "Yeah, man. I heard you talking to someone and I heard him, but there wasn't anyone there."

"Congratulations," Ron beamed, "you are one of the few who has heard the audible voice of God." Jimi looked puzzled. "Are you familiar with the baptism of the Holy Spirit? Have you accepted Jesus?"

"Oh, that religion shit. I don't believe in that crap," Hendrix replied.

Jimi didn't believe in organized religion. He felt that the spiritual message had been lost to power struggles and greed. Jimi considered himself spiritual, but not religious.

~ **Ron Russell** ~

The Murder of Jimi Hendrix

As Monika Dannemann recounted in her book titled **the inner world of Jimi Hendrix**, "Jimi explained that he felt the Church had knowledge and wisdom, but that this had to be given in the right way to the people. Much of what is said is right, but seems false. He thought that the Church concealed too much, had distanced itself from the people it wanted to reach, and was not effective in putting across the message of God to the people."

Ron Russell had come to a similar conclusion years before.

"The voice told me that we have something in common," Ron continued. "Did you ever know Dr. Martin Luther King?"

Hendrix replied, "No, I didn't. I always wanted to meet him. He was one of my heroes."

Ron stated, "Well, I used to be his best friend so that's not it. Have you heard of the Revelation Fires?"

Jimi recalled, "I have a favorite aunt who told me about a thing that happened in Chicago Heights when she was a teenager. Her name is Martha Brown."

The Murder of Jimi Hendrix

"That's it," Ron exclaimed. "That's what we have in common. Let me tell you the story and you tell me if it's the story you heard." Ron related the story of the young child who had been visited by the Holy Spirit, spoke in tongues, and began an association with the Pentecostal Church of God. The event fostered a lifelong friendship with Martha Brown, the aunt of Jimi Hendrix.

"I am **The Child**," Ron said.

"That's the story," Jimi said with a look of wonderment.

Martha Brown played a pivotal role in the lives of both Ron Russell and Jimi Hendrix. It was Martha who explained to Ron the meaning of what happened to him following his extraordinary experience in Chicago Heights so long ago. Martha had had a similar trip through the Revival Fires, speaking in tongues and the Baptism of the Holy Spirit.

The Murder of Jimi Hendrix

The two musicians forged an immediate and deep bond. Their spirits spoke to each other exchanging a lifetime of experiences and emotions in a minute. The two began talking about music and influences. Jimi described his concept for a new band that would fuse the elements of Jazz, Classical, Gospel, and Rock together.

"Jimi wanted to develop, expand, and move on in many fields. In 1969 he intended to change and develop his music, but unfortunately faced strong opposition from his manager, who tried to make Jimi repeat the style of music which initially had made him famous; more '*Hey Joe*' and 'Purple Haze'. Michael Jeffery tried to persuade Jimi to stay in line and do what he was told to do. Persuasion meant any means necessary, including strong threats," related Jimi's girlfriend, Monika Dannemann.

Ron described his early history, from the time he had first seen Gene Krupa and knew that he wanted to be a drummer, through the years of jazz lessons and countless hours of practice, to the jam he was playing that day.

The Murder of Jimi Hendrix

Jimi invited Ron to join him into the limousine where they could continue their talk in private. Once in the limousine, Jimi pulled out his "works" (drug world slang for equipment used with heroin). Ron looked on in horror as he watched his new friend "shoot up" to ease his tension.

The previous night, Jimi put on a disastrous show where he disgustedly threw down his guitar and left the stage. Cindi Halisky, wife of legendary keyboardist Mark Halisky, recounted, "We were all very disappointed. We'd anxiously anticipated the show and it was nothing. He was terrible. He was obviously *on* something."

"Man, that stuff is no good, Jimi," Ron advised. "Where'd you get that?"

"I got it from that skinny guy out there," Jimi pointed out Albert Ronald "Ron" Wells standing in the crowd.

~ **Ron Russell** ~

The Murder of Jimi Hendrix

Ron Russell rocketed out of the limousine and took after Ron Wells. "He was faster than I was then. He's lucky, 'cause I would've done bodily harm to little Ron if I'd have caught him," Ron Russell recalls now.

Years later, in 1994, Ron Russell and I met up with Ron Wells. Upon hearing Ron Russell speak of his days with Hendrix, Ron Wells interrupted to say, "Hey, you were the guy who was going to kill me because I gave heroin to Hendrix." It turned out to be the last heroin that Jimi Hendrix ever did. Unfortunately, it wasn't the last for Ron Wells. "He was crispy bacon when I met him."

"Jimi was a mess when I met him," Russell related.

Ron Russell returned to the limousine and coaxed Jimi to the stage for a jam with Raindriver. The music that resulted was incredible. The hippies received a preview of the future of Hendrix' music. As Ron remembers the moment, "It was Of God. It was incredible." The feeling transcended the local scene propelling all who attended to a new plane where music combined with spirituality.

The Murder of Jimi Hendrix

Famed keyboardist Brad Trumbull remembered the day, "Every Sunday I would roll my B3 & Leslie out of my van onto that stage and jam with whoever came up. I was young and just learning, building my resume. It was awesome to add Jimi Hendrix to the list."

Hendrix felt it too. Memories of the debacle of the previous evening disappeared as Jimi began playing with a greater joy and purpose than he had in his recent memory. "The dream that he had of combining Jazz, Classical, Rock, Blues, and Gospel together was flowing from his guitar and was complimented perfectly by the musicians on the stage," Ron recalled.

It was clear that they were destined to play together. Jimi invited Ron to join his new group, which would be called **The Jimi Hendrix Fusion Band**. Naturally, Ron accepted.

"… Jimi was looking for new musicians to work and play with. His dream was to find good players who would also be his friends, which was the reason he chose Billy Cox as a new bass player when Noel Redding left the band," Monika Dannemann reported.

~ **Ron Russell** ~

The Murder of Jimi Hendrix

After the jam session, Ron spoke to Jimi in earnest about the heroin. "Man," Ron spoke, "if we're going to be together I want it to really fly. Man, we've got to get you off the stuff."

Hendrix listened to his new friend intently. Though they had just met they felt as if they had known each other forever. Jimi knew inherently that he could trust Ron, unlike the plethora of parasites that sought him out for his fame and fortune.

Ron invited Jimi to stay with him at his humble abode in Tampa where Hendrix could kick the ugly habit that was ruining his life and his talent. Jimi agreed.

Jimi moved in with Ron. The first days were the worst. Jimi was wracked by tremors as the physically addicting drug grudgingly loosed its hold on him. Ron recalls cradling a shuddering Jimi in his arms on the floor.

The Murder of Jimi Hendrix

Ron soon perceived that Jimi's problem was due as much to exhaustion as to heroin addiction. Jimi described how his manager, Mike Jeffery, continually pressured him to produce more, tour more, record more… Everything was more, more, more.

As Monika recalled, "He also told me about the stress and exhaustion he felt after two and a half years of constant touring all over Europe and America, plus recording on top of this. He said that he needed a holiday for a long time, but that his manager, Mike Jeffery, kept on booking new tours, often without first informing him."

Jimi and Ron talked at length about life, death, spirituality, and, particularly, music. They jammed together for hours on end. They also wrote several gospel songs together.

~ **Ron Russell** ~

The Murder of Jimi Hendrix

"You see, Jimi was a funny guy. When he was alone he didn't listen to rock and roll. He'd listen to Classical, Jazz, and Gospel. He really loved Gospel music," Ron recalled. "When Hendrix wrote music, he'd hear the whole thing. He couldn't read a lick of music, but he'd play each instrument in the orchestra's part. He'd play something and say, 'I want the violins to play this,' and so on. He was really remarkable in that way."

Jimi described his love for Monika Dannemann who he called his soul mate. He confided that he worried that his love for Monika being discovered and exploited by Mike Jeffery.

Kathy Etchingham met Jimi in September of 1966 upon his arrival in London. They had a whirlwind love affair. Kathy inspired several Hendrix songs. After a bitter argument, he wrote *The Wind Cries Mary*. On a better day, *Foxy Lady*. They had a solid relationship for three years. While on the road, Jimi wrote *Send My Love to Linda*, which was originally named *Send My Love to Kathy*, but she objected to being named in the song. By 1969 they drifted apart, which opened the door for Monika Dannemann.

The Murder of Jimi Hendrix

Monika's testimony concerning Jimi's death changed several times and is generally considered unreliable and raises more questions than it answers.

However, Monika's description of Hendrix's mood does ring true, "Jimi didn't feel safe anymore, and he also felt unable to protect me from anything that might happen. He told me to wait for him, and that he would come as soon as he had sorted out everything with his manager. He wanted to break free from his management first and then join me in England.".

In the last two years of Jimi's life, several suspicious events fed Jimi's paranoia.
In May 1969, he was arrested at Toronto Airport for carrying drugs, which he believed Jeffery had planted to retain control.

Death threats and other attempts to intimidate Jimi followed. He was kidnapped by purported Mafioso only to be miraculously rescued by Michael Jeffery.

It was clear to Ron that Jimi desperately wanted to change his management situation, but his manager had neatly tied Jimi in legal entanglements.

~ Ron Russell ~

The Murder of Jimi Hendrix

Jimi listened intently as Ron Russell told of his friendship with Dr. Martin Luther King from their first meeting in Melbourne, Florida in 1962 until Dr. King's murder in 1968. Ron confided to Jimi the incredible sense of loss that he felt following Martin's assassination.

Jimi confided to Ron that some "heavy shit" had been happening around him, that he feared for his own safety. Hendrix told Ron that Mike Jeffery was constantly making deals behind his back attempting to control the superstars every movement.

Jimi asked Jeffery to shorten the tour Jeffry claimed the money was needed because Electric Lady Studio was draining the finances. In reality, Jeffrey was the drain. He was siphoning revenue to pay his own debts to mobsters. Quite simply, losing Jimi would result in death for Jeffry. It became a matter of Hendrix or himself.

Jimi was defiant. He took steps to free himself of what amounted to modern day slavery.

The Murder of Jimi Hendrix

Jimi Hendrix found himself in a position familiar to musicians like "Little Richard", Chuck Berry, Billie Holiday and a host of other talented folks who had a genius for music, but were ignorant of business machinations. The underhanded tactics of managers like Mike Jeffery were beyond the imagination of creators like Hendrix until it was too late.

Days passed, Jimi's tremors receded, and he started feeling healthy again. In their extended discussions of the upcoming Jimi Hendrix Fusion Band, he asked Ron whom they should use as their bass player. Jimi loved Billy Cox, but knew that the pace and pressure that had severely weathered Jimi would surely crush Billy. That prophecy came true during the European Tour.

"You see, the bass and drums have to be together," Ron explained, "They are the foundation." Ron thought immediately of his friend Wally Dentz. Wally was a premiere bass player, a natural musician, who ultimately joined the Bellamy Brothers and has become known as their third brother.

~ Ron Russell ~

The Murder of Jimi Hendrix

Jimi had been trying to recruit a keyboard player that he had met in his early days of club gigs in London. Keith Emerson was the enigmatic keyboard player for the band Nice. Emerson was fascinated with Jimi's concept of fusing disparate musical elements together. However, Jimi was unable to extricate himself from his current contractual obligations. Keith eventually joined forces with former King Crimson bassist and lead singer, Greg Lake, and The Crazy World of Arthur Brown drummer, Carl Palmer, to form the infamous classical rock group Emerson, Lake & Palmer.

The players for the Jimi Hendrix Fusion band were set: Jimi Hendrix on guitar and lead vocals, multi-talented Wally Dentz on bass, and Ron Russell on drums. Both Ron and Wally are good singers. Jimi was thrilled with the prospect of three-part harmonies

At the end of his stay, Jimi Hendrix was clean. He had wrestled the monkey from his back. He hadn't felt that good since his days as guitar man with the Isley Brothers. He looked forward to a future that would see him moving in new musical directions.

The Murder of Jimi Hendrix

Hendrix worked a grueling schedule in 1969 leading up to the pinnacle show of his career at Woodstock where he played 17 songs in the set, returning to play *Hey Joe* as an encore. His output fell off after that: 7 songs at Lennox Avenue, New York on September 5th, recorded two songs at ABC Studios in LA on September 9th, recorded 3 songs the very next day at the Salvation in Greenwich Village, NY, (ever fly coast to coast?), a forgettable set at Jai-Alai (pronounced Hi-Lie) in Miami, Florida on the 21st, a disastrous show in Clearwater on the 22nd where threw down his guitar in disgust and chastised the audience, which a pregnant Cindi Middleton Halisky (wife of legendary keyboardist Mark Halisky) remembered as hugely disappointing. He met Ron Russell the next day.

A month later, Jimi was free of all addictions for the first times in years, except for one. Music. Creativity skyrocketed, songs were flowing swiftly, his inventiveness returned. He was eager to follow his exciting new path. But first, he had to make some money. Electric Lady Studios was an enormous drain on his cash resources. And strong suspicions that manager Michael Jeffrey was stealing vast sums ensured that Jimi would not be signing a new contract. Jimi agreed to play a short tour of Europe to immediately raise necessary cash.

~ Ron Russell ~

The Murder of Jimi Hendrix

Jimi invited Ron to drum for him on the tour, replacing Mitch Mitchell who Jimi saw as limited in his abilities as a drummer. Mitch was a highly excitable individual, prone to violent outbursts if crossed. Ron had several confrontations with Mitch and, "they weren't pretty," according to Ron. "We almost came to blows on one occasion."

Unfortunately, Ron didn't have a passport and there wasn't sufficient time for him to secure one before Jimi's final European tour began. Ron had to pass on the offer, a fact that haunts him to this day. Had he accompanied Jimi on tour perhaps Jimi would not have died.

Jimi was left with but one alternative: do the tour with his old drummer Mitch Mitchell.

Mike Jeffery feared people like Ron Russell because they threatened his hold on Jimi. Jeffery didn't like Jimi to have friends who would putting ideas in his head and giving him strength. He preferred Jimi to remain isolated. The only people allowed close were those that Jeffery could use to influence and manipulate Jimi. He gleefully promoted the conflicts between Mitch Mitchell and Ron Russell. He was manipulating Mitch, too.

The Last Tour

Jimi Hendrix left for the European tour. There was much prep work to do: rehearsals, booking venues, lining up hotels and transportation, and a myriad of tiny details. Usually, Jeffrey's people took care of those details, but Hendrix was determined to take back control of his career and life.

Jimi called frequently to talk to Ron Russell about song ideas for the album that they would record when he returned to the States.

Jimi sounded very happy. He had met a jazz pianist in Minneapolis, Minnesota that he invited to join the band. He jammed with Bobby Lyle, as he had with Ron, and thought him the ideal fourth member to complete the band.

Ron's heart could feel the change that had come over his friend. Jimi wrote a dozen or more new tunes during the tour. He would play and sing them over the phone. His playing took on a new purpose as well, as if he was already playing with the new band.

September 18, 1970

In the early morning hours of September 18th, 1970, Ron Russell was teaching a Head Start class at Manhattan Middle School in Tampa. Ron's best friend, Martin Luther King, created the Head Start program. Ron felt a duty to forward his friends vision, "I had thirty little black kids there and they were all precious."

Early that morning, the principal of the school came down to get Ron.

"Jimi Hendrix is on the phone for you?" His voice belied his initial disbelief that the *real* Jimi Hendrix was calling the school.

Ron smiled and said, "Cool. It's OK, he's a friend of mine."

Jimi sounded very good to Ron's ears. Hendrix was in London at the flat of his girlfriend and new soul mate, Monika Dannemann. Jimi was in good health and spirits, excited about the future.

The Murder of Jimi Hendrix

Jimi and Ron talked for a few moments about the upcoming sessions at Electric Lady Studios in New York. Jimi would be returning to New York in a few days and was eager to get his new band into the studio. Ron and Wally Dentz were ready to fly to New York to join their friend and new boss.

Suddenly, Ron heard a familiar voice enter the London flat.

The mood quickly turned ugly. "Is that that fucking drummer from Tampa," Ron recognized the voice as that of Mitch Mitchell. "You tell him that he's never gonna record with you. He's never gonna play with you. He's never gonna get any money out of you."

The hair on Ron's body stood on end in alarm. Ron felt a terrible wave of dread. "Jimi, get out of there, man. I'm getting' a bad feeling about this."

Hendrix laughed off Ron's warning, "Ah, don't worry about him, he's just crazy. I've handled him before." Ron heard wrestling in the distant room.
Before Ron could respond he heard Jimi cry out, "Ouch. Man, he just jammed me in the temple with a needle."

~ Ron Russell ~

The Murder of Jimi Hendrix

Ron cried out, "Jimi?"

Ron heard the telephone receiver fall to the floor and Hendrix with it. He could hear Jimi choking and vomiting. Ron was horrified. He felt helpless. He was an ocean away and couldn't help his friend with whatever was happening to him. Ron came to a sickening realization: he was listening to his friend die a horrible, agonizing death.

Then, Ron heard the voice that he had immediately recognized moments before, the voice of former Hendrix Experience drummer Mitch Mitchell. A second voice said to Mitch, "Get those pills and jam 'em down his throat."

Michael Jeffrey confided to James "Tappy" Write that he ordered Mitch to pour wine down Jimi's throat as he twitched on the floor in the last moments of his life.

The Murder of Jimi Hendrix

In an interview, Tappy expanded, "The second point is that both the ambulance drivers and the doctor who attended Jimi at the hospital say that Jimi was in a real mess. Dr. John Bannister was the surgical registrar on duty that day. When Dr. Bannister read my book, he wrote to me from Australia: 'The very striking memory of this event,' he wrote, 'was the considerable amount of alcohol in his larynx and pharynx… I recall vividly the large amounts of red wine that oozed from his stomach and his lungs.'

Yet the toxicology report revealed an alcohol blood level equivalent to about four pints of beer – and in any case, Jimi had an unusually low tolerance to alcohol."

"As a person regurgitates they naturally inhale and influx anything in their throat," Ron described. Mitch Mitchell and Michael Jeffrey were setting up the cover story:**Rock Star Dies Of Overdose**.

And then, there was silence.

Nothing more was heard from Jimi Hendrix. For a time, Ron heard no sound from the London flat save for some shuffling and dragging sounds, confused voices.

~ Ron Russell ~

The Murder of Jimi Hendrix

At the other end of the wire Ron was pleading, "What is going on? Jimi? Jimi? Are you there? Are you alright?"

Jimi didn't reply.

After a desperate eternity, the receiver was picked up. Ron absolutely identifies that it was the voice of Mitch Mitchell.

"**The nigger is dead!** And I'm coming for you next," Mitchell coldly stated.

In shock, Ron responded, "Come on. I live in Tampa, Florida. I'm waiting for you." Then, the line went dead.

Ron was confused, dazed, shocked. What had just happened? Could it be true? Did he just hear his good friends' murder? What should he do? What could he do?

Aftermath

Ron immediately called Martha Brown, Jimi's aunt, the connection that they had in common. He described to her what happened. Martha was shocked by the news. She excused herself to call Jimi's father, Al Hendrix, with the tragic news. Ron expected that authorities would contact him for his statement about the murder. He was never contacted.

"I can't say for sure who the other person in the room was, but I strongly suspect that it was Michael Jeffery," Ron states. "I can't prove that Jeffery was there,"

"But I can prove that Mitch Mitchell murdered Jimi Hendrix!"

It makes sense that if Michael Jeffery could exert the kind of control that Monika and others have described over a mega-star like Jimi Hendrix, that Mitch Mitchell was powerless to refuse to do his bidding.

The Murder of Jimi Hendrix

Mitchell's income source would dry up, as well, if Jimi made his intended change in musical direction. With Jimi dead they had enough material recorded to release Hendrix albums for decades.

That is in fact what happened. Jimi Hendrix holds the dubious distinction of having released the most posthumous albums of any artist.

To normal folks this would seem a shortsighted approach at best, to literally kill the goose that was laying the golden eggs. Jimi Hendrix had already revolutionized the world of rock and roll as well as the art of guitar playing. Had he just been allowed to follow his own inspired course he surely would have continued to lead rock in new directions. After all, isn't that what really made him the star that he was?

The Murder of Jimi Hendrix

Mike Jeffery was far from typical. He bragged that he had served in the British Secret Service. He fancied himself as a James Bond, a secret agent for M126. He told all who would listen that he was a specialist in all sorts of devious tactics. He claimed to know all the tricks of the trade. He claimed to have killed before. Early on in his career he had purported connections with the Newcastle crime scene. He had become involved with the New York Mafia. He was deeply indebted to mobsters. If he lost Jimi's revenue, he would be killed.

Immediately after Jimi's death, Jeffery promoted the story that Jimi Hendrix, like other rock stars of his generation, had died of a drug overdose. Just another rock star that got too high, a black man who sang about voodoo. Jeffery could depend on the fact that officials wouldn't look too closely for foul play in this matter.

Michael Jeffrey didn't underestimate the indifference with which authorities would treat Jimi's demise even though the physical evidence did not support the manufactured story. It was just another dead entertainer in London.

The autopsy reports the discovery of an "unknown substance" in Jimi's blood, but no narcotics and a minimal blood-alcohol level.

~ Ron Russell ~

The Murder of Jimi Hendrix

Ron Russell states that, "they injected Jimi in the temple, behind the hairline." A normal autopsy would not have discovered the tiny puncture mark obscured by Jimi's thick Afro. "I believe that whatever that unknown substance was, that it is what killed him," Ron declares.

Michael Jeffery's MI-6 training came into play that day. He was a trained assassin, calmly, coldly executing a deserter.

Ron Russell fell into a deep funk of nearly overwhelming depression. Another close friend had been murdered. A little over two years before on April 4th, 1968, Ron's best friend, civil rights leader Dr. Martin Luther King, had been murdered. Ron had been devastated by Dr. King's assassination. And now, he had lost his dearest friend, Jimi Hendrix.

Ron drew within himself fearing to get close to anyone lest they be murdered too.

The natural question is: Why didn't Ron speak out about this murder sooner? Why did he remain silent for so many years?

The Murder of Jimi Hendrix

The answer is quite simple: The pain of remembering was too great. Ron buried the memories deep within his mind. Ron suppressed his memories for over 25 years.

Ron has a very successful career going as percussionist for Men In Blues, voted the best blues band in Atlanta for many years running, and many other prestigious gigs.

Going public with his murder allegations leaves Ron with nothing to gain and literally everything to lose. **Perhaps, even his life.**

~ Ron Russell ~

The Murder of Jimi Hendrix

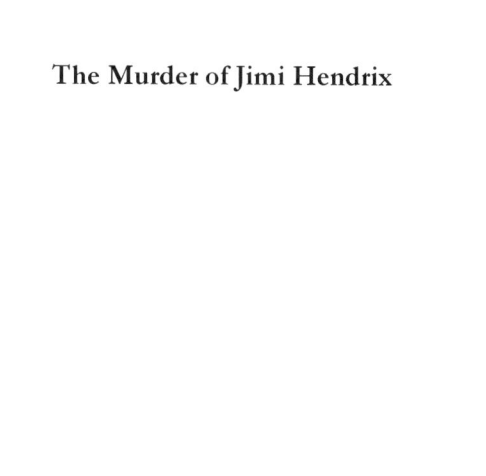